MW01644345

Memories Matter

Understanding emotions and helpful advice for
Alzheimer's and dementia caregivers

DAWN BRENNIMAN WIRTZ

Memories Matter

Understanding emotions and helpful advice for Alzheimer's and dementia caregivers

© 2025 by Dawn Brenniman Wirtz

All rights are reserved. No part of this publication may be reproduced in any form or by any electronic or mechanical means, including information storage and retrieval systems, without permission in writing by the publisher, except by a reviewer who may quote brief passages in a review.

Layout by Abhisar Design

Cover Design by Two Mile High Marketing

First Edition: March 2025

Acknowledgments

I want to thank my husband, Troy, for always encouraging me and loving me throughout this writing process.

I want to thank my dad for being the best caregiver for my mom. Thank you for loving her and caring for her with such dignity.

I want to thank my kids, Brittney, Austin, Mason & Molly, and their significant others for supporting the Alzheimer's cause and their grandmothers. It's been beautiful to witness.

I want to thank my sister, Suzy, for helping me carry on our childhood and family memories for Mom and Dad.

I want to thank Laura for joining me (by phone) on every caregiving drive I've taken since January 2024. Calling me both ways and spending at least an hour on the phone with me keeps me going. The laughter, the tears, the distractions!

I want to thank my "girls": Micko, Jenny, Amy, Tricia, and Lisa for making time for me during my caregiving visits to hang out again, like our high school years!

I want to thank Aunt Betty, Uncle Jim, and Uncle Tom (Mom's siblings) for always being there for their big sister (and all of us).

I want to thank Kelly and Two Mile High Marketing for being the name that popped up when I googled "How to write a nonfiction book" and for leading me through this process of writing and publishing this book.

I want to thank my Author Power Circle ladies. Meeting every Tuesday since November 2024 and supporting each other during the writing of our books has been a gift.

I want to thank Erika for accommodating my work schedule so I can be gone four days each month for my caregiving visits.

I want to thank Marla for asking who my mom was and always listening and caring about a woman she'd never met.

I want to thank everyone who inquires and comments about my mom through Facebook, donates to the Alzheimer's Association, and supports the cause.

Lastly, I want to thank my mom for being my mom. Thank you for always loving me. You still show your love for me even in the depths of this horrible disease, and for that, I am forever grateful.

Foreword by Lauren Livingston

As the Communications Director for the Alzheimer's Association Iowa Chapter, I've had the privilege of hearing stories from countless Alzheimer's and dementia caregivers over the past 5 years. Though everyone's story and experience are unique, they also always have two things in common—caregiving for a loved one living with Alzheimer's or dementia is incredibly challenging, and it is vital for caregivers to ask for help along the way. Dawn Wirtz mentioned both of these things when I talked with her for the first time about her caregiving journey too.

I connected with Dawn after she signed up for a media spokesperson training I hosted for our volunteers because she was interested in sharing her voice and story of helping her father care for her mother with Alzheimer's disease. As Dawn mentions in her book, she's been involved in many ways over the years with the Alzheimer's Association, and we are so lucky to have her as a walker, fundraiser, volunteer, and advocate for all those facing Alzheimer's and dementia.

The first thing I asked Dawn to help with after the spokesperson training was to write a letter to the editor to help promote the Walk in Des Moines. As she has in this book, she so eloquently wrote about the grief a caregiver feels watching a loved one go through this disease, how it's OK to have these feelings, and how she still tries to appreciate every moment she has with her mom, even though the moments may be very different from before the disease started to progress. Here is a small piece of what she wrote in her letter:

"I discovered that by organizing a team, fundraising, and preparing for walk day for several months, I can channel some of my grief I have with losing my mom slowly to this disease. I miss the daily phone calls I used to have with my mom and how involved she was in my life. My walk involvement helps me feel connected to Mom in a different way."

When Dawn asked me to first read a draft of her book and then write the foreword for it, I was incredibly honored, and after reading through it the first time, I knew she had written something very special. I'm proud of the work I do at the Alzheimer's Association, and the organization does a great job of providing free resources to families facing the disease, and hope that a cure is just around the corner. But it's not always easy for a large organization to connect on an individual level with a dementia caregiver and help them feel seen and validated when it comes to the complicated emotions they may face. Dawn's book, however, does just that. Her explanations of ambiguous grief and how honest she is about grappling with these feelings while also trying to put on a brave, happy face when she's with her mom are so powerful. I know so many dementia caregivers will read this and feel so understood and relieved that they aren't alone.

As someone who hasn't had a direct caregiving experience, this book has given me a much better understanding of the reality of caregiving and helps me with the work I do every day. I've dealt with chronic pain due to a health condition for the past 5 years, and I was able to relate and find helpful insights throughout this book related to my situation as well. It can also help nondementia caregivers understand how they can be a better support system for the dementia caregivers in their lives. This book will help anyone who reads it have more empathy and understanding of what it means to be a dementia caregiver.

This book is such a beautiful, heartbreaking, relatable, and important story, and it fills a gap that helps describe and explain the full scope of caregiving, including the parts that are hard to discuss with others. As the number of people living with Alzheimer's or dementia continues to grow, more and more people will take on the insurmountable role of being a caregiver to their loved one living with the disease. This book will be there for them to explain, validate, and justify all the complicated emotions they will face on their caregiving journey. Whether you are a dementia caregiver now or in the future, know a dementia caregiver, or have experienced complicated feelings of grief, this book is for you.

Contents

Introduction

I Have a Book in Me

"Memories of our lives, our weeks, and our deeds will continue in others."

—Rosa Parks

According to the Alzheimer's Association, "Alzheimer's is a fatal and progressive disease that attacks the brain, killing nerve cells and tissue, affecting an individual's ability to remember, think, plan, and ultimately, function. Alzheimer's is the most common cause of dementia. Brain changes associated with Alzheimer's may begin 20 or more years before symptoms appear."

Alzheimer's disease has also been described as "the most terrifying illness on the face of the earth." According to Alzheimer's Disease International, as of March 2023, there were more than 55 million people with dementia worldwide, and this is expected to almost triple by 2050 to an estimated 132 million. People with Alzheimer's disease live, on average, about 8 years from the onset of symptoms but can live up to 20 years. Caregiving for persons with dementia is typically done in their own homes by family members and other unpaid caregivers. Dementia often progresses slowly, so a third of caregivers provide care for 5 years or longer.

When I was 10 years old, I wrote a story for a contest in school about my maternal grandmother living in a nursing home with Alzheimer's disease. When I was 16 years old, my paternal

grandmother was diagnosed with Alzheimer's disease. In college, I minored in gerontology and completed internships at the Alzheimer's Association Des Moines Chapter and at a memory care facility in Des Moines. After graduating from college in 1994, I spent 20 years working in retirement communities, continuing to have a great deal of experience with those inflicted with Alzheimer's disease or dementia. I was instrumental in opening a memory care neighborhood in one of the assisted living facilities where I worked. As early as I can remember, I was drawn to working with older people, particularly those with dementia and especially Alzheimer's. I was well educated and had several decades of hands-on experience under my belt when this disease hit as close to home as possible.

In 2018, my mom was diagnosed with Alzheimer's disease, and everything I've known about Alzheimer's for nearly my whole life didn't seem to help. By that, I mean I've always known the facts, the what-to-do, what-not-to-do, the hows, and the how-nots as far as caring for and interacting with someone with Alzheimer's disease. These past 6 years since Mom's diagnosis, I have struggled with so many new emotions. I am grieving the loss of someone who is still alive, which is so painful and confusing. As a result, I have been searching for just the right book to help me process these emotions and validate the grief, loss, guilt, and sadness I feel every day. During one of my therapy sessions, as I was sharing these frustrations and emotions with my therapist, I said, "I think I might have a book in me," and she agreed.

There's often a struggle to be a caregiver to a loved one and manage those feelings of sadness, anger, loss, and guilt so that you can be a thoughtful and present caregiver. People with Alzheimer's can still read and feel your mood and often mirror it. I've found if I am anxious, sad, or irritated around Mom, she picks up on that, which impacts her mood. I work hard at being calm, gentle, encouraging, kind, loving, and happy around her. When I'm helping with her incontinence, assisting with her shower, or interacting with her stuffed animal, "Miss Piggy," it's extremely difficult to exhibit those positive emotions when I also feel the negative ones.

While I do have to push down those negative emotions at certain times, I also know it's imperative that I still express them at other times. I must get them out. I want to discuss them with others who are going through similar situations. I want to have those feelings validated. I want to normalize these emotions and start conversations about them. I want to replace the belief that "at least she's (the person with Alzheimer's) happy; that's all that matters" with memories matter.

The purpose of this book is to be a source of comfort and validation for those caring for a loved one with Alzheimer's disease*. This is an emotional book about the painful journey of losing a loved one slowly and grieving them while they are still alive. This book will validate the difficulty and complexity of this disease. It will discuss different types of memories and why they are all important. This book will define ambiguous grief and show how it fits in with Alzheimer's disease. It will emphasize the importance of keeping the past of your loved ones alive while celebrating who they are today. This book will provide many ways to practice self-care while caring for and loving someone with Alzheimer's disease. Lastly, at the end of each chapter are questions for you, the reader, to ponder and space to journal your thoughts.

*For this book, the term "Alzheimer's disease" will be utilized, but it includes all forms of dementia.

Chapter 1

Alzheimer's Is Difficult and Complex

"Memory is the diary that we all carry about with us."

—Oscar Wilde

The facts of Alzheimer's disease are staggering. The Alzheimer's Association reports that "There are nearly 7 million Americans age 65+ living with Alzheimer's dementia. Some 62,000 Iowans live with Alzheimer's. One in 9 people aged 65 and older have Alzheimer's disease. Currently, more than 11 million family members and friends are serving as Alzheimer's caregivers. There are 98,000 caregivers in Iowa." Those are a few of the most common facts of Alzheimer's disease.

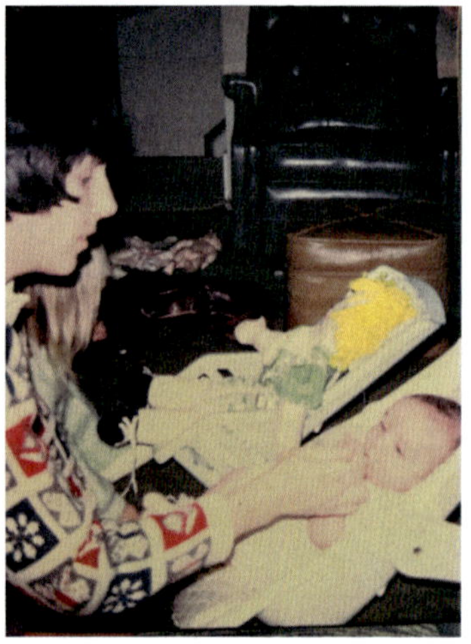

My facts are this: My mom, Kathleen Ford Brenniman, was born on November 29, 1942, in Dearborn, Michigan. She is the oldest of four children. She has an undergraduate degree, a master's degree, and a law degree. She was married on August 28, 1965, to Gary Russell Brenniman. She is a mother of two and a grandmother of four. She is a liberal feminist who has always fought for equal rights for women. She has read hundreds of books in

her lifetime, loves all kinds of music, and has hit many golf balls over the years. She also can't tell you any of these facts about herself. Her memories of herself are gone. Her 52 years of memories of me, her youngest daughter, are gone. I have become her "friend" who she "likes very much," or sometimes, I'm just a nice person; it depends on the day.

Alzheimer's disease creates layers of grief, loss, and sadness for those caring for and loving the person afflicted with it. I've often pondered, what if none of us had memories? What if we looked at an old photo and felt nothing? What if we didn't know where we went to college? What if we didn't know our children's names and where they lived? What if memories didn't matter?

The T-shirts I had made for the Alzheimer's Walks to honor my mom in 2023 and 2024 say, "*Memories Matter*" on the front. In late 2024, I watched Ellen DeGeneres's newest standup, *For Your Approval*. She shared that her mom, suffering from Alzheimer's, doesn't know Ellen is her daughter anymore. Ellen then goes on to say, ". . . at least she's happy. That's all that matters." I've heard that said regarding someone with Alzheimer's before. However, this time, it made me sad and really ponder that statement. We know that those with Alzheimer's can, at times, be combative and angry, so when someone with Alzheimer's is happy and content, we believe we should be grateful. And believe me, we are, but we don't have to be just grateful. I am slowly learning that even though my mom is extremely happy and agreeable most of the time, I experience moments of sadness, loss, and anger. I then experience guilt because I should be grateful since she is happy. Nothing else should matter, but to me, it all matters.

One of the most difficult parts of Alzheimer's is watching the person lose their memories. Dementia is caused by damage to the brain, which can affect areas of the brain involved in creating and retrieving memories. For a person with dementia, memory problems will become more persistent and will begin to affect all aspects of everyday life. This becomes difficult to cope with for both the person

themself and the people around them. Even though we don't want our loved ones to progress in their disease, when they know they have this memory loss, the pain is even more profound for all involved. I've experienced many tearful moments with Mom recognizing that she is sick or saying "sorry" for something she did or forgot. As I wrote this book in the fall and winter of 2024, we were past this stage, as she often didn't recognize her memory loss anymore.

Before we dive deeper into memory loss with Alzheimer's disease, it's essential to understand some of the basics of memory loss. Everyone is affected differently, but many people with dementia experience some of the following (provided by the Alzheimer's Association):

- **Forgetting recent conversations or events** (often referred to as short-term memory loss): During a 10-minute phone conversation with Mom, she will often ask me the same question at least 2 to 4 times.
- **Struggling to find the right word in a conversation:** This can create frustrations for the person struggling and the person listening. We try to be as patient as possible with Mom and let her try to find her words, but if it's causing her too much distress, we gently suggest a word to help her.
- **Forgetting names of people and objects:** When your loved one begins to forget family members' names, the pain is real. It's important never to quiz your loved one or try to "work them." This is the progression of the disease. While writing this book, I was with Mom, sitting with her after we had decorated the Christmas tree, and out of nowhere, she asked, "What's your name?" Then she asked, "How old are you?" and then, "Where do you live?" In those moments, it's hard to be grateful that Mom is happy because I'm feeling the loss of the woman who gave birth to me in January 1972, named me, and helped move me to Iowa in 1990.

- **Losing or misplacing items** (such as keys or glasses): This can be an early sign that your loved one may have more serious memory loss. With the use of cell phones now, misplacing a cell phone is so common. This was the item that Mom lost the most. It can be so frustrating for the person. Patience in helping them locate their item(s) is crucial.
- **Getting lost in familiar surroundings or on familiar journeys:** This is tricky because if the person is alone, they may not let you know that this happened out of embarrassment. I'm not sure if Mom had a lot of trouble with this when she was still driving. I will share in a later chapter about how COVID-19 impacted her ability to drive and go places alone.
- **Forgetting how to carry out familiar tasks** (such as making a cup of tea): Several Christmases before Mom was diagnosed, we noticed that putting together the holiday meals was not going as smoothly as it used to. Frustration became a regular part of these celebrations for many years.
- **Forgetting appointments, birthdays, or anniversaries:** I'll never forget my birthday in 2019 when Mom and I were still having our daily talks on the phone on my way to work, and Mom did not mention my birthday. Some of these losses hit harder than others, and this was one of them. As the disease progresses, you become accustomed to knowing that your loved one is going to need to be prompted to say that it's your birthday, and you're just grateful they still recognize you when they lock eyes with you.
- **Not being able to keep track of medication and whether or when it has been taken:** Dad has been in charge of Mom's medications for many years now.
- **Struggling to recognize the faces of people they know well:** This is even harder than forgetting the names of people, and I have seen this happen with Mom. Luckily, I am visiting and FaceTiming Mom enough that my face is very recognizable to her, and I can tell she knows me when we lock eyes, and she breaks out with a

big smile. With this disease, we know it's just a matter of time until she won't be able to recognize my face.

These changes may be more visible to family and friends than to the person themselves, which is why many people are reluctant to get tested, as they are unaware of these issues. As I mentioned, Mom was diagnosed in November 2018. We had tried to talk her into seeing a doctor for a few years before without any luck and with much resistance. When the early signs begin, it's easy to try to ignore or make excuses for what is happening. Overall functioning is still there, so why would we want to discover such devastating news? My sister and I would gently bring it up to Mom and Dad, and it met with continued resistance until the fall of 2018, when they both agreed. Early diagnosis is important so that medications can slow the process and accommodations in your loved one's life can begin. There have been many advances in research and medications, which will continue to occur. While the news is devastating if confirmed, I firmly believe that early testing and diagnosis are important. I was tested in June 2024. I recognize that my issues with my memory at that time were related to anxiety and the grief of seeing my mom progress in her illness. I have since felt peace of mind from my testing and will continue this throughout my life as needed.

Most people know that those with Alzheimer's struggle with repeating themselves and short-term memory loss, but it goes so much deeper than that because we are dealing with memories of a life lived. When I sit next to Mom on the couch with my laptop, doing some work for my job, Mom will ask, "What is it that you do?" While I'm answering that question again, my heart is breaking. Mom no longer remembers that I graduated from Drake University in 1994 with a degree in sociology and a minor in gerontology. She doesn't remember that I went back to Drake in 2015–2018 to get my master's in Mental Health Counseling and that I'm working as a therapist now. Mom lived through those big moments in my life with me, but her memories of my huge milestones are gone.

The questions I posed earlier in this chapter about memories are painful because my mom doesn't know any of those answers. Mom lives in the present. She lives in the 5-minute (or less) present. Being with the person who raised you and was present for all your big and small moments in your life and not being able to reflect on those together or have a conversation about your kids or your job or anything else is a kind of pain that needs to be discussed. It's not enough for me that Mom is physically healthy and happy. I want more. I want my mom. I want those phone calls we had on my way to work every day for years and years. I want to hear her opinions (even the ones I didn't like hearing!).

My mom was an attorney for the City of Evanston, Illinois. She was an English teacher first but decided she wanted more when she was 38, and I was 8 years old. I have so many memories of Mom being gone during her law school years. I always wrote stories about her being gone and left them on her bed to discover when she got home from a late night of studying. Even though I didn't like that she was an attorney when I was younger, I came to respect it as I grew older and even benefited from her knowledge. Mom really knew her stuff. She was a brilliant and respected attorney. While writing this book, I've also been thinking more about Mom as an English teacher. Throughout my high school and college years, Mom was also my go-to for proofing my papers. We didn't have the technology we have now, so I depended on Mom to give it that "expert look-over." As I approached the part in my writing process to have this book edited, the irony of it all came flooding back to me. Mom would be the person to read this book. The book I'm writing about her she cannot read. This is how this journey works. You never know when you're going to be struck with the pain of a loss.

Mom had beautiful handwriting; the old-school cursive that was pretty with loops and circles and curls. During Thanksgiving 2021, I got out an old (1997) article about hosting your first Thanksgiving that Mom mailed to me. At the top of the article, she wrote, in her old-fashioned cursive, *"Hope this helps. Love, Mom."* I was struck that day by her handwriting, which I hadn't seen in a while, as Dad had taken

Thought this might be helpful. Love, Mom

Holiday help

Timing is everything

Cook dishes ahead and let someone else fill the water glasses

By William Rice
Tribune Food and Wine Columnist

over signing cards for the past year. Two months later, for my 50th birthday, I got the *"Love, Mom"* tattooed on my left forearm. I forever have her pretty cursive handwriting with me.

In August 2024, during one of my caregiving visits, I bought a card for Mom to give Dad for his birthday. I wanted her to still have the normalcy (and me too) of signing the card and writing on the envelope. I wrote each letter for her to copy and guided and encouraged her through the process. The result was heartbreaking,

Credit: NMK Photograpy

as you can see in the photo. This woman, who would brilliantly argue her cases in court, could no longer write her letters. Her pretty, old-school, curly cursive handwriting was gone. Her knowledge of the alphabet was gone. Her ability to copy what she sees on paper was gone. Despite the sadness it brings to my heart, I continue to give her the opportunity to pick cards for Dad and sign them. I can look at my left forearm, see her handwriting, and remember all the cards and letters she wrote me over my lifetime.

My examples and memories of Mom continue to show how devastating this disease is and how it's not as simple as "at least she's happy." As family and caregivers, I believe we must acknowledge this devastation while recognizing and appreciating that our loved one is happy. In this journey, I am learning that it's a tricky balance.

I thought witnessing the difficulties with Mom trying to write was hard, but I had no idea what I was getting into by helping with her incontinence and showering her. Again, this disease has so many more layers than repetition and forgetfulness.

In 2022, Dad had the upstairs tub and shower turned into a walk-in shower, making it easier for Mom. Eventually, Dad began to share that Mom needed some help with cueing in the shower. Cueing involves stating each step that needs to be done and pointing to the object at the same time. Soon after, she needed some hands-on help. In March 2024, during one of my caregiving visits, I offered to help Mom with a shower to give Dad a break. I observed one shower first with Dad helping, and then I was on my own. We are blessed that Mom is so agreeable to accepting help from us. It certainly made the logistics of doing her personal care easier. The emotional part

was not easy, to say the least. In that first shower experience, it was hard not to think of this as a full-circle moment. Fifty-two years ago, she was bathing me, and now, here I am, bathing my mom. Despite the emotional difficulty in this, she and I have showering down to a pretty good science. I shower her every time I visit. I now get in the shower with her as she needs more than just cueing. When she covers her eyes with the washcloth, and I wash her hair, she often takes it down, and we have a few "peek-a-boo" moments and laugh. Dad always mentions hearing so much laughter when I help her in the shower! At that moment, I can laugh and be playful with her. Later at night, when I'm tucked in bed and reflecting upon my day, I cry. It's a tricky balance of being present in those moments, regulating the tough emotions, and finding time later to acknowledge the grief and sadness.

These emotions and thoughts I'm sharing are likely felt by the 98,000 caregivers in Iowa, along with many others worldwide. These are not new feelings. I'm hoping that it will become more normalized and comfortable to share these feelings. Some of these emotions might be shared in Alzheimer's support groups, but I want us as caregivers to feel comfortable sharing these when anyone asks, "How's your mom doing?" We shouldn't have to answer, "Well, she's happy and healthy, and that's all that matters." We should be able to say just how it is without carrying guilt along with it. When people who have recently seen my mom say to me later, "Wow, your mom really is doing so well," I feel like I've been punched in the gut hearing that. They don't mean it that way, but they aren't looking at the whole picture. They are seeing her smile and how healthy she looks. They don't see how she doesn't know that the toilet paper goes in the toilet and is not rolled up in her hand. They don't know she talks to her stuffed animals and carries them around. They don't know she can't sign her name. They don't know she uses her toothbrush to brush her hair. They don't know she thinks I'm her friend. They don't know she thinks the high school I attended is her high school. They don't know that she doesn't know how to use a napkin anymore when she eats. Put together, those things don't feel like Mom is doing well.

As a caregiver and a daughter who loves her mom so much, I do want people to know these things, not to get sympathy or to embarrass my mom, but to educate and normalize. We understand what chemotherapy does to a person with cancer. We know what happens when someone is in hospice at the end of their life. We talk about those things. Let's talk about how someone with Alzheimer's is really doing. I truly believe my mom would want that. In the early stages of her disease, she did not shy away from letting people in her circles know what was going on. She stopped leading the Latina Conference through her women's group after 11 years and told them why. She stopped playing in the bell choir after 35 years and told the church why. She wasn't doing well, and she wasn't embarrassed. She shared her story, and I'm continuing to do that for her, as she cannot anymore.

I started writing this book in October 2024, the first year that I started my caregiving visits. Those visits made me even more aware of Mom's changes, behaviors, and actions. During my December caregiving visit before Christmas 2024, I witnessed Mom do something that immediately brought extreme sadness to my heart. Still, I could look at it differently because I was writing this book. Dad was making breakfast, and she was waiting in the living room. As I have mentioned, Mom loves stuffed animals. She has many that stay on the recliner that she sits in. I saw her arrange them all in her recliner, talking to them as she often does, but this time, she started rocking the recliner like she was rocking a baby. She was saying gentle and quiet words to them that I couldn't make out as I was down the hallway. I immediately felt sadness watching her with these stuffed animals, but later, as I was processing that moment, I realized what I had witnessed. I got a glimpse of what my mom was like with me when I was a baby. We don't have memories of being held, rocked, or soothed by our parents when we're babies, but I felt like that's what I witnessed. I took the sadness of watching her play with her stuffed animals and saw the gentle and nurturing side of her.

Writing this book and the additional time I spend with Mom has helped me look at her actions and behaviors differently. It doesn't always happen right away, and sometimes, I'm unable to. Sometimes, something I see is just too devastating, but at other times, I can bring some different meaning to it. I think of this moment now, of Mom rocking her stuffed animals, and I see it as a gift. I witnessed something that most people don't get to. You must look hard, but sometimes, you can find blessings in this horrible disease.

This chapter shared the devastation of Alzheimer's disease. This chapter shared that the disease goes way beyond repetitiveness and forgetfulness. It introduced you to my past mom and present mom—two very different people. It introduced you to some raw emotions in my journey. If you are a caregiver, I challenge you to identify your emotions in your journey. I encourage you to help educate others and share your feelings when the opportunity presents itself. If you're not a caregiver, thank you for choosing this book to help educate yourself, read my journey, and learn more about this disease. I challenge you to ask different questions to those caring for a loved one with Alzheimer's disease. I encourage you to look beyond the smile and appearance of the person with the disease and ask about the past and present person standing before you.

Reader Application

- What connection do you have to this book?
- What are you hoping to get out of this book?
- How can you apply this chapter to your situation or experience?

NOTES:

Chapter 2

Why Are Memories Important?

"Memory is a way of holding on to the things you love, the things you are, the things you never want to lose."

—from The Wonder Years

Do you think memories are just about our past and don't have much other purpose? Chapter 1 asked, "What if none of us had memories? What if we looked at an old photo and felt nothing? What if we didn't know where we went to college? What if we didn't know our children's names and where they lived? What if memories didn't matter?" Chapter 2 will share that there are different types of memories and many reasons why memories are important. This chapter will reveal that everyday memory provides richness and meaning to our lives. We have memories surrounding the transition between childhood and adulthood. We have involuntary memories as well as autobiographical memories.

Alzheimer's disease can affect memory in several ways, including: difficulty creating new memories, difficulty and inability retrieving information, and impaired smell recognition.

When younger adults think about memories, they might remember their college years when they were required to learn and retain a lot of information for their classes. In college, success depends on how well one remembers, which can be optimized with

study techniques that increase attention and understanding of course material. As a result, outside of college, they may not "fully recognize the value of everyday memory that occurs outside the realm of academic achievement" (Belli, Robert).

The years between our childhood and adulthood are packed full of a novelty of experiences and so many firsts, including first job, first romantic relationship, first college course, and first apartment. These experiences are well remembered due to their novelty. This explains why older, healthy adults can hold on to these memories. These older memories can be the last memories to go in Alzheimer's disease. We often refer to these as "long-term memories." I recently discovered, by looking at old (64-year-old) photos with my mom, that her

long-term memories and short-term memories are gone. I knew my mom had a boyfriend in high school, and we stumbled across a few photos of them at school dances. I was hopeful his name might pop up in Mom's memory, but it did not. On another occasion, Mom and I were driving past my old high school, and she spoke up and said, "There's my high school" (which, of course, it wasn't). Mom's first experiences in her young adulthood are gone.

Involuntary memories are memories we are not intentionally trying to remember. They pop into our minds independently from a scent, sound, song, or sight. Most of the time, these involuntary memories are of pleasant past events. They are involuntary "in the sense that we are not intentionally trying to remember; these memories seemingly pop into our minds on their own" (Belli, Robert).

Sometimes, in the car, I can tell that an Elvis song might jog a little something in Mom's involuntary memory. She might sing some lyrics when I play a song from *The Sound of Music*. I can tell her involuntary memories are fading as well.

Autobiographical memories are often shared through storytelling. We often share these memories with our friends and family. Robert Belli shares that "such remembering of mutually experienced past experiences or even telling friends of an experience that was uniquely one's own, is one way in which we develop stronger friendships." These memories also serve us by helping us better understand our current life situation "through the constraints and opportunities the past has placed on us, and the directions that we would like to pursue for our future" (Belli, Robert). A sign of Alzheimer's disease may be a parent sharing the same story repeatedly at a family gathering. As this disease progresses, the stories are not only shared less, but they are eventually forgotten. I challenge you to remember this when someone older shares something you have heard so many times. I challenge you to be patient and enjoy their story anyway, as someday, they may not be able to tell it at all.

Jessa Claire identifies reasons why memories are important in her article in *UpJourney* on March 21, 2024. Jessa shares, "Memories are bits and pieces of our past that we carry with us—sort of like the playlist of our lives. Not only do memories keep us connected to our past, but they also do so much more for us than simply looking back. This is important to recognize when we care for those with Alzheimer's disease who not only are not connected to their past anymore, but they also lose all the other benefits of memories.

As we explore the many benefits of memories that Claire identifies, keep in mind that those with Alzheimer's disease no longer have these benefits and recognize how that adds to the complexity of this disease and drastically changes who they are.

1. **Memories Shape Our Identify:** Memories include our past. They include places we've been, people we've met, foods we've tried, and mistakes we've made. Think of how often you make a choice

today based on a past experience. I know I will not eat cooked carrots because I remember how much I disliked them as a child, and I know that hasn't changed for me. We avoid certain things, or we choose to do certain activities based on past experiences. Mom is allergic to scallops. If I made those for dinner for her, she would eat them, as her ability to remember that experience when scallops made her sick is gone.

2. **Memories Connect Us to Our Past:** Memories help us look back at what we've been through in our lives and help us see how we've changed over time. Old photos allow us to remember how we felt back then. I can look at the day I moved into my freshman dorm at Drake University, August 1990, and remember exactly the fear and anxiety that I felt at that moment of my choice to move 325 miles away from home. Looking at that photo now, I can see how much I've changed since then and be so proud of myself. Mom no longer feels those emotions while looking through old photos.

3. **Memories Guide Our Future Decisions:** Memories can be like blueprints for us. They play a huge role when we must choose what to do next. Past successes and failures are important for us to remember and use as guides. Mom's blueprints are gone, and she's unable to make any future decisions anymore.

4. **Memories Help Us Empathize with Others:** Did you know that memories can make us kinder and more understanding toward others? They can make our relationships stronger and interactions in these relationships more compassionate and caring. Mom cannot share memories and emotions with others any longer. She has lost many relationships during her disease progression.

5. **Memories Contribute to Our Overall Mental Health:** Memories can help us become stronger and more able to handle life's challenges. Memories can make us sad but also help us to handle difficult times in the future. Memories can remind us that we are not alone and that others have similar experiences and feelings. I often see Mom's frustration when she can't find the words she

needs. I imagine how alone she must feel in those moments and how this adds to her frustrations and anger.

6. **Memories Fuel Our Creativity and Imagination:** Memories can inspire us to new ideas and creativity. We can pull from our past experiences and even use those to solve problems. When I do a craft with my mom, without these memories fueling her creativity and imagination, she often struggles with what color to use or where to glue something. I use a lot of encouragement and praise during our crafts to help relieve her frustrations.

7. **Memories Help Maintain Social Bonds:** Closeness with others is about spending time together and sharing memories. These shared moments help keep the relationships strong over time. Since I started my caregiving visits in January 2024, I have reconnected with my high school friends, who I've been living apart from for over 30 years. While we have lost contact for many years, our shared high school memories have kept our relationships strong over these past decades. As you can imagine, many relationships are lost when one has Alzheimer's disease.

8. **Memories Keep Traditions and Culture Alive:** These traditions help keep us connected and give us a sense of where we come from. While my sister and I have tried to keep some of our holiday traditions the same as Mom always did, we have made minor adjustments as needed. We will make the Christmas punch with the cherry ice ring for the grandkids (now all adults), but it's still not the same as when Mom made it.

9. **Memories Contribute to a Sense of Belonging:** Claire shares that memories are like "invisible threads that tie us to our community, friends, and family." We create a "we" feeling when we share memories that make others feel included. As Mom's disease has progressed, she can't follow when friends or family share, "Remember when . . .?" Mom will, on occasion, go out to lunch with the three women she used to golf with. They are still golfing, and they try to include Mom in a lunch every now and then. Mom

used to be an integral part of this foursome, but now, due to her dementia, it's hard for her to belong to this group anymore.

10. **Memories Influence Our Behavior and Attitudes:** Memories can help shape our behaviors and attitudes and give us clues on navigating life. Without these memories giving clues, Mom's behaviors and attitudes are not always age-appropriate anymore. On one occasion, in a mall food court, Dad gave Mom a cup of lemonade, and she began to play with her straw and make silly noises with it. Dad had to tell her to stop, and she began to pout. More childlike behaviors are very common as Alzheimer's disease progresses.

11. **Memories Support Language Development:** Our ability to speak and understand language is closely linked with our memories. Words, phrases, and sentences are stored in more memories. Without this, it is hard for Mom to recall and tell stories and even recall and use specific words.

12. **Memories Foster a Sense of Accomplishment:** Memories help us remember our wins and achievements. They're like little trophies that remind us of what we have achieved and what we still can achieve. They help us feel successful and can motivate us to reach future goals. Mom is a highly accomplished woman. At times, she'll remember she was an attorney, but most of her accomplishments in her nearly 82 years are no longer in her memories.

Some believe focusing on memories might seem like you're not living in the present. In her article in *UpJourney*, Jessa Claire showed us that memories are not only about the past. Memories help us in the present and prepare us for what comes next. Memories can make us smarter and help us understand others better.

The next time you're caregiving or communicating with someone with Alzheimer's disease, remember how complex memories are and how much someone is missing without having those. Sometimes, Mom will try to say something to me, and I can see the frustration

on her face. She'll look at me and say, "This is really hard." It's so important we never forget how hard it is for them.

While someone with Alzheimer's disease clearly struggles with their memory, it's still vital to make memories with them and surround them with social opportunities. COVID-19 was a time in our history when isolating ourselves was how we thought we could protect ourselves from the spread of the virus. In particular, many elderly people were socially isolated, and those with all types of dementia progressed in their disease. Further research is needed to understand why COVID-19 accelerates brain deterioration in patients with dementia. Still, I can reflect on these COVID years with Mom and identify how the pandemic changed her.

As stated before, Mom was diagnosed with Alzheimer's disease in November 2018. When the pandemic hit in the early spring of 2020, Mom was still driving, playing bell choir, playing golf in the summer, going to their health club, reading, going to movies, and using her cell phone. When the pandemic shut things down, my parents had very little to do. Being very active and physically healthy, they moved their exercise routine from the health club to walks outside. Their health club and movie theaters shut down, the church went virtual, they weren't going to eat with their many different groups of friends, and they had very few, if any, places to go. As a family, we prioritized virtual calls, but I could tell the pandemic was wearing on them, especially Mom. During this time, there was less for them to do, and Mom was getting more repetitive in our phone calls. She also didn't drive for many consecutive months, and then when golf was going to start up later that summer, my sister and I expressed some concerns about Mom driving.

During that summer, we had difficult talks with Dad about not letting Mom drive anymore. Eventually, in the fall of 2020, Mom was no longer a driver. When the bell choir started again, Mom was bringing her bells and music home to practice during the week, as this was becoming harder as well. Christmas 2020 was the first Christmas we didn't get together as a family. I remember it being such a difficult decision, but COVID was on a surge, so we canceled it

in person and did it virtually. We bought and mailed gifts to each other and did a virtual gift opening. Of course, we all know that Christmas is so much more than the gift opening. We missed out on the cooking, the gathering together, the physical touches, and the laughs in person.

The COVID impact trickled throughout the end of 2021. I struggled with the changes in Mom. She wasn't posting on Facebook anymore. It was hit or miss if she'd answer a text. We were still making our morning calls on the way to my job most mornings, but the repetitiveness weighed on me. Mom was different, and I was feeling less connected to her. I tried to start each phone call by being more patient, and I would find myself in the same frustrating situation that I was in the day before. I found myself cutting the time for our phone calls.

In the early spring of 2022, the changes in Mom were taking their toll on Dad. He wasn't ready to have any assistance in the house, so a compromise was found at ESSE Adult Day Services in Glen Ellyn, Illinois, near Mom and Dad's home. The Latin word *esse* means "to be." Their "purpose is to acknowledge and support the continuing life, growth, and fruitfulness throughout one's life span." At ESSE, they encourage their participants "to be all that they can be by providing opportunities for socialization and meaningful activities in a caring environment."

While finding ESSE was ultimately a positive part of our journey with Mom, at first, it was hard to accept that she needed to be in an Adult Day Care Center. It added to the difficulties I was having accepting the progression she was having in this disease. The guilt and negative feelings about myself grew and grew throughout 2021 and into the end of 2022. I accomplished a great deal of work with my therapist during those times. As soon as I thought I was in a better place with Mom, at the end of 2022, I recognized a shift in her Alzheimer's disease that suddenly took me on a new path in this challenging journey.

This chapter helped you recognize how important memories of all kinds are. It identified that memories are complex, and when all sorts of memories are lost, your relationship with your loved one is difficult. As I shared in this chapter, memories shape and connect us. Without these, relationships can suffer. I work hard at making sure Mom and I are still connected. However, we don't have much to talk about these days. We can't reminisce together, but our moments together are still meaningful. I just have to work a little harder at it.

Reader Application:

- What are some of the first experiences in your young adult life that come to mind?
- What involuntary memories come to your mind when you hear a particular song or smell a specific scent?
- What story is shared on repeat in your family?
- How do you feel when you hear it over and over?
- How would you feel if you never heard that story again?

NOTES:

Chapter 3

What Is Ambiguous Grief?

"The life of the dead is placed in the memory of the living."

—Marcus Tullius Cicero

During this shift in my difficult journey, I learned a new term to describe how I felt that I wasn't even familiar with yet. The phrase "ambiguous grief" has been coined by researcher Dr. Pauline Boss. The phrase describes a situation where a loved one is with us physically but is no longer psychologically or emotionally present for one reason or another. A typical example of ambiguous grief is grieving a loved one who is suffering from Alzheimer's. The loss of someone who is still alive is considerably different from someone dying, in large part because there is no closure. Ambiguous grief is a type of complicated grief that involves longing and confusion. When there is a death, you're more likely to get support from family and friends, along with eventually finding closure through traditional mourning rituals and the natural grieving process. These unique kinds of losses and grief that you may feel toward a loved one who is still alive are often not recognized, acknowledged, or understood by the people around you. This can add to your grief and the loneliness you are feeling.

Kenneth J. Doka shares that "Grief has been identified as the 'constant yet hidden companion' of dementia. As caregivers, we often experience a continuous and profound sense of loss as we are living through the changes associated with the progression of

Alzheimer's. We are also grieving the losses occurring in our own lives. The loss of the way the relationship used to be."

In October 2023, we were finally out of the depths of COVID-19, and my parents were visiting me in Iowa for some family birthdays. We moved to this home in February 2021. Mom and Dad had visited us here many times in the year and a half we'd been here, so I felt like I had been punched in the gut when I overheard Mom quietly ask Dad, "Whose house are we in?" I felt a shift in me at that very moment. I suddenly felt like what I was doing for Mom (phone calls and occasional visits) was not enough. It felt like it was not enough for her, not enough for me, and certainly not enough for Dad, her full-time caregiver.

After that visit, I proposed a plan to my dad. Starting in January 2024, I would make two caregiving visits a month, Thursdays to Saturdays. I needed to balance being with my parents and still being with my family on weekends. I was fortunate to work out this schedule with my job. Even with making a job switch in the middle of 2024, I could continue this schedule.

During 2024, I adjusted to these caregiving visits and the ambiguous grief that was growing deeper for me. If you're familiar with Alzheimer's disease at all, you know that the progression does not stop, and it often feels like it's picking up speed. That is what I felt when I heard Mom ask my dad, "Whose house are we in?" I felt like 2024 was also the year of watching the deterioration and losses. Another massive loss for Mom (although she was not aware of it) was taking off her wedding rings in January 2024. Dad was so worried that she would lose them with all the fidgeting she was doing with them. I devised an idea to lotion her hands, and we removed her rings. I slipped them to Dad without Mom watching, and he put them away for safekeeping. She has never asked for them again. While she was unaware this happened, I still see it as a loss for her. She's worn those rings for 58 years. At that moment, I was sad for Dad, sad for Mom, and sad for having to take off Mom's rings.

During one of my March 2024 caregiving visits, Dad asked me to pick out some Depends for Mom to start using instead of underwear. He felt overwhelmed picking them out, so he asked me to do that. Dad explained that Mom was beginning to have some incontinent issues, and he thought it was time for this next step. As we geared ourselves up for this next step in our journey with Mom, I began recognizing how agreeable Mom was to these changes. She was no longer wearing the underwear she was used to wearing for 80 years. It was now Depends with an extra pad. I then purchased reusable underpads for her bed and chairs/couches she uses at home so Dad doesn't have to do so much laundry. I bought pastel colors and let her choose which one she wanted for her bed, and she was actually excited about it. While that response can be heartbreaking, I decided to be grateful for her excitement and agreement in this next step in her incontinence. By April 2024, Mom was never alone in the bathroom.

It was mostly Dad caregiving for her, but occasionally, I would help or my aunt or my sister or a caregiver at the adult day center Mom started attending in 2022. As I was working hard in my own therapy to understand ambiguous grief and try to begin to "meet Mom where she's at," I was starting to feel grateful at certain moments during this difficult journey. I was grateful to take Mom to the restroom, as she was typically agreeable and cheerful.

She began some interesting bathroom rituals with toilet paper, pulling up her Depends, and drying her hands. At the beginning of these new bathroom rituals, my heart hurt, and I sometimes had to look away. As it became "our norm," I embraced these moments. I could manage my sadness while finding some joy and laughter in them. This is a perfect example of changing your mind-set from an "either/or" to a "both/and." I used to believe, "I either love my mom with dementia exactly as she is now, OR I miss how she used to be." Now, I lean toward "I love my mom with dementia exactly as she is now, AND I miss how she used to be."

Dealing with ambiguous loss is difficult, but shifting the way you think about ambiguous loss can be helpful. My mom lost a lot about

herself in 2024, but she hasn't lost everything about herself. I can look for things that are still my mom. She still has a sense of humor, and we can still laugh together. She does have an emotional part to her. In September 2024, I hurt my ankle, and while she got confused and rubbed my arm, she sat beside me for a long time. She rubbed my arm, showing her concern for me and asking if what she was doing was helping me. I have learned to embrace those moments and feel joy and happiness rather than sadness or anger.

Another tricky part about loving and caregiving for someone who has changed so considerably into a different version of themselves during this disease is the use of present and past tense when you talk about them. I had a client come into her session carrying a Harry Potter book. I immediately shared, "Oh, my mom used to love Harry Potter!" When I hear myself use past tense about my mom, it feels like she's not there. What I said was the truth, though, since Mom doesn't even know who Harry Potter is anymore, and she can't read anymore. As I've been describing Mom the way she is today, you likely are not picturing an educated, liberal, healthy, and strong older woman in her early eighties.

In September 2024, I was shopping in a local gift shop that I'd frequented many times and chatted with the owner, Marla. She happened to have some small purple decorative pumpkins. I picked up about 6 of them, glanced at the register toward her, and said, "These are perfect!" I continued to share how I would use them as centerpieces for the family lunch I was hosting after the Alzheimer's Walk in a few weeks. I mentioned that Mom has Alzheimer's, and she and Dad were coming that weekend. As she listened intently to me, when I paused, she so gracefully asked, "What was your mom like?" I was struck by how she used the past tense, not because I was offended, but because, at this moment, she was recognizing that Mom likely was not the same woman she once was. I was also struck by her interest in who my mom was instead of how she was doing right now. I miss the Mom she was, and I love to talk about that woman. I gathered my thoughts and shared, "My mom was a brilliant attorney. She was a liberal feminist who always believed in

and fought for equal rights for women. She loved to play golf and was so competitive." I shared a few other things and left that moment feeling happy and fulfilled that I got to share about my mom today. Not the mom who is sick, but the mom who I used to know.

Ambiguous grief has been defined in this chapter. Now, I will provide specific tips for coping with this grief, along with examples of how I have used each.

1. **Feel the pain:** This may sound like a horrible tip, but denying your feelings only intensifies and prolongs this grief. During my caregiving visits, after I tucked Mom into bed in the evening, I took my shower and simply stood there under the hot, running water and felt the whole day, especially the pain. During the day, I don't allow myself to feel all the pain because I need to be present with Mom and not let her see or feel my pain, as she can still recognize emotions.

2. **Cry:** This often can cooccur with tip #1. As I'm feeling pain from the day, the tears usually come at the same time. This can be a very therapeutic moment, cleansing and relieving the pain from the inside. I also do this many other moments when I am not with my mom. Crying is something I frequently use to help with my grief and express my emotions.

3. **Talk:** It can be helpful to talk to a therapist, a trusted friend, or someone outside your family. A support group through an organization such as the Alzheimer's Association may also be a promising avenue to provide the opportunity to talk to others on a similar journey. I see my therapist on a bimonthly basis, and I have a dear friend who calls me in the car on my way to and from Mom and Dad's for every single caregiving visit. The support I feel in those calls provides the strength I need before and after these visits. It's also an outlet for my emotions.

4. **Keep a journal:** A journal provides a private place to explore your emotions without interruption. You can improve your mental health and well-being by journaling your experiences

and thoughts. We will explore 10 different types of journaling in Chapter 5 about self-care, along with some excerpts from my journal that I currently keep.

5. **Consider your own needs:** If you are a caregiver who spends a great deal of time with your loved one, taking regular breaks can keep you in touch with the outside world, raise your morale, and recharge your batteries. Dad is the one I worry about more with this one. He uses the days Mom goes to ESSE, her adult care day center, for his breaks. I constantly check in with him to see if he needs to add additional days a ESSE, as mom's care is getting harder.

6. **Find comfort:** This can be different for different people. Many people find comfort in rituals like prayer, meditation, and other activities. I choose walks, scrapbooking, and long, hot baths with lots of bubbles and candles.

7. **Be kind to yourself:** This includes being patient with your feelings. It's about balancing the happy and sad, the angry and peaceful, and the guilty and glad. Be patient with yourself. I struggle so much with sad days. I've started labeling it "Alzheimer's sad" so that people around me know I'm having a hard day regarding Mom.

8. **Learn to laugh again:** Finding joy and happiness in life can be one way to honor the happy times you used to share with your loved one with dementia. I have pictures of Mom during different stages of her life taped on the mirror in my closet. I look at her every day and laugh at some of the memories. It also helps that Mom loves to laugh and can still find humor in some things. Despite the difficulty of these caregiving visits, Dad, Mom, and I share many laughs I would have missed had I not been doing this. The laughter helps me feel gratitude in times I otherwise would not.

The goal of dealing with ambiguous grief is to learn to live with it by finding meaning rather than seeking closure. Consider the following:

- **Naming the problem:** In this case, the experience is caregiving for a loved one with Alzheimer's and losing them while they are still physically here. If we name the problem as "ambiguous loss," the coping process can begin. Earlier in 2024, I was unfamiliar with this specific term. I was naming it grief, but it didn't feel right since Mom is still with us. Knowing there is a term for what I'm feeling provides me with validation and comfort.
- **Resilience:** Increasing your tolerance for ambiguity can help build resilience. Feeling more comfortable going between past and present tense with Mom helps me feel stronger in this journey.
- **Finding meaning:** Recognize that it's possible to find meaning in this experience, no matter how confusing it is. Finding meaning is the main topic of my next chapter.

This chapter has been essential to help you understand your type of loss. Once you understand it, you can describe it, and it can be easier to communicate what you're experiencing. It may also make it easier to reach out for help. I challenge you to identify some of the tips listed in this chapter to help you cope with your ambiguous loss. I challenge you to find meaning rather than seeking closure.

Reader Application:

- Have you ever experienced Ambiguous Grief before?
- If you have, are there any of the 8 tips to coping with this grief that you can apply in your life today?
- Can you think of a difficult situation and try to shift your mind-set about it?
- Can you recognize something positive in it while still acknowledging the difficulties of it?

NOTES:

Chapter 4

How to Celebrate Amid Memory Loss

"Each day of our lives, we make deposits in the memory banks of our children."

—Charles Swindoll

Mom grew up in a conservative household where her dad was a Republican. Mom grew up to be a liberal Democrat. I love the story she used to tell when her dad came to visit her in 1972 and saw all her campaign materials for George McGovern. She knew he wouldn't be happy, to say the least, but she didn't hide who she was, even after McGovern ended up losing to Richard Nixon in one of the biggest landslides in U.S. electoral history. I had been thinking about this story during the 2024 election. Thankfully, with the Mental Capacity Act and Dad's power of attorney, Mom could still vote. I share this story to kick off this chapter about celebrating and finding meaning amid memory loss. Mom is no longer involved in election campaigns, but she voted in the 2024 election despite having advanced Alzheimer's. I think that's something to celebrate.

You can celebrate your loved one by engaging them in some activities. As a caregiver, you can try to tap into the emotional strength of memories while creating meaningful moments. You can talk about past experiences that may bring up memories. Stephanie Thurrott, a contributing writer to Banner Health Blog, put together a list of ideas, and I've added comments on what I've tried with Mom.

- **Look at old recipes or cook or bake together:** Christmas 2023, Mom and I made her "famous" punch with the cherry ice ring for the grandkids (now all adults), just as she has done for 25 years. Christmas 2024, my sister and I made it due to Mom's decline, but we made sure she drank some!
- **Flip through photo albums:** Mom and I do this at every caregiving visit. Dad has several of their photo albums accessible to Mom on the coffee table near her favorite chair. My sister found a photo frame called Skylight with Wi-Fi, and the whole family can send photos and videos to the frame anytime.
- **Rewatch a favorite movie:** I recently put on *The Sound of Music* for Mom. While following shows has become more difficult for her, putting on old favorite ones gets some of her attention. I can't even tell you how many times she and I have watched this movie together in our lives!
- **Encourage them to share stories from the past:** We could do this in the earlier stages of Mom's Alzheimer's. If they can do this, I would encourage it for as long as possible, even if you've heard the story numerous times. I promise that you will miss it someday.
- **Listen to music or play musical instruments:** When Dad takes her on drives to the arboretum, he always has on Elvis Radio. Familiar songs bring joy to them both. I've witnessed it during my caregiving visits when I'm along for the ride.

- **Work in a garden:** I had Mom pick tomatoes from our garden when they visited during the gardening season. We simplify gardening at their home now and get summer-

and fall-potted flowers for their front stoop. It brings Mom joy whenever she's in and out of the house.

- **Visit places that used to be part of their routine:** Sunday church and lunch, which are still part of Mom's routine, as are the arboretum and a few walking paths. When Dad says they're going to the arboretum or church, Mom is familiar and comfortable with that plan.
- **Plan visits with small groups of family members or friends:** Every Sunday, they go to church, and then Mom and Dad go out to lunch at the same restaurant with the same group of friends and sit in the same spot with the same waitress. Mom benefits from living in the same town (and home) for 50 years, so she still has many nearby friends. Dad plans lunches and dinners with friends, which Mom still enjoys. These interactions with their friends also benefit Dad as the primary caregiver.

While engaging your loved one in these activities, I've added tips on how to help these activities go smoothly, along with more examples from my journey with Mom.

Focus on ability, not limitations: Focus on what your loved one can still do and celebrate their remaining strengths and skills. When I plan meals for my parents during my caregiving visits, I choose ones Mom can help make with me. I also choose meals that aren't challenging to eat, like spaghetti noodles or tacos, as certain types of food become more challenging to navigate as the disease progresses.

Involve your loved one: Find ways to involve your loved one. When I wash the dishes after meals, I have Mom wipe down the table and dry some dishes. She still wants and needs to feel useful and necessary. Once, when I went upstairs to start setting the table and making the salads, I didn't bring Mom with me right away from downstairs. Apparently, I waited too long because she snuck up on me in the kitchen! She had remembered that I went upstairs to do something, and she wanted to be involved.

Honor traditions: Even if your loved one can't remember it's their spouse's birthday or their anniversary, honor those important traditions anyway. I've shared how I make sure I take Mom shopping for cards for Dad for his birthday, Father's Day, and their anniversary. It's important for both of them that these traditions are continued.

Be with them in their world: This can be one of the more challenging ones. Trying to bring them back into reality feels more natural, but correcting a loved one's mistakes leads to more confusion and frustration. Helping your loved one enjoy their present moment can bring more happiness and comfort. As mentioned in an earlier chapter, Mom has a favorite stuffed animal. She has several, but Miss Piggy is her favorite. Our whole family has done a fantastic job accepting that Mom/Grandma has stuffed animals she talks to and engages with. We have accepted this as part of Mom's world and have joined her there.

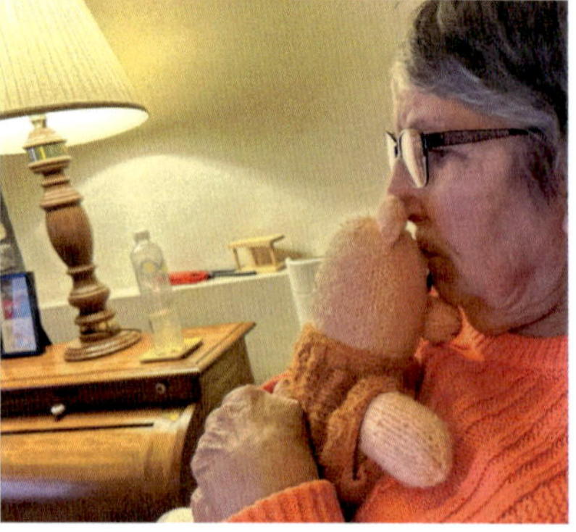

Another way to celebrate your loved one is to form a team in their honor, raise money, and participate in your local Walk to End Alzheimer's event. Throughout my life, I have participated in this walk more times than I can remember. I've volunteered, been a committee member, and been a walker. The last two years have been the most meaningful to me as I created *Team Kathy* for mom. The Des Moines

Walk to End Alzheimer's is always the last Saturday in September. In the summer of 2023, I talked my family into walking together (it wasn't hard to talk them into supporting grandma!). I ordered purple shirts with the saying, "*Memories Matter #endalz*," and on the back, *Team Kathy*. Dad was on board to travel to us for the weekend to honor Mom. Walk 2023 was a success! The family

was together, the sun was shining, and Mom walked the 2-mile walk like the champion she was.

We celebrated afterward with a special luncheon at our home. As Mom deteriorated more in 2024, I wasn't sure if the walk was going to be possible again for my parents. I casually told the family that whoever wanted to walk in the 2024 walk could walk, and I wasn't going to make it a big "to do." Immediately after I put the message out in the family group text, the kids responded with support, "We'll be there!"

Dad and I discussed the trip. He wanted to do this for Mom, so we decided to do the 2024 walk! The biggest change was having a wheelchair on hand, as the 2-mile walk would be more demanding for Mom this time. Another change was that Team Kathy grew in 2024. I made more special touches on the lunch with all-purple decorations and cookies with "Team Kathy" on them. There's no question that Mom felt the love all day and all weekend. The amazing result of celebrating your loved one is that you, as the caregiver, also feel that. For two years in a row, I threw myself into creating a special walk weekend for Mom, from all things purple to fundraising on Facebook (we raised $5,030 in two years) to thank-you notes afterward, and finally, a photo book from the day for Mom.

The power of celebrating a life that you wish was going in a different direction is extraordinary. It changes the pain and despair into joy and gratitude. It puts a hold on the grief. It lifts you up and puts you on a different journey for that moment, and then those memories are there.

Another way we celebrated Mom in a big way was when she retired from her church bell choir after 35 years. As I mentioned in Chapter 2, during the fall of 2020, Mom was bringing her bells home for extra practice. By Christmas 2022, it was time for Mom to hang up her bells. Her disease was really taking its toll on her abilities to read and play music. We knew Mom deserved a special send-off, as being a part of something for 35 years is no small feat. In early December 2022, we knew she'd be performing for the last time. We got as much of the family available to make the drive and surprise Mom at church. The pastor also did a short presentation thanking Mom for her decades of service to the bell choir. I have found that big celebrations are so crucial amid this ugly disease. Big celebrations take away some of the pain in those moments. The person experiences so many losses during this disease. Just like driving, Mom knew why this activity was ending for her. Her awareness in 2022 of what this disease was taking

from her was still so great. That makes the pain for all of us so much more profound. So, celebrating, creating surprises, and doing big things is a way to help all of us in our grief.

One last example of celebrating cannot be left out of this book. It's a little out of order, as this was January 2019. Dare To Dream: Get Educated! Latina Conference was an event that Mom was on the board of for 11 years. This conference is designed specifically for Latina girls, often focusing on middle-school age, where the primary aim is to empower them by highlighting the importance of education, career opportunities, and personal development, encouraging them to pursue their goals and "dare to dream" about their future. Key points of this conference focus on education, empowerment, and mother-daughter involvement.

Typically held in January of each year, Mom's last conference was in 2019, just a few months after she was diagnosed. As noted throughout the book, most of Mom's losses started in 2020. There weren't many changes we saw in Mom before 2020. Still, because this involvement in the conference was so detailed and focused throughout an entire year, she struggled throughout 2018 regarding it and reluctantly decided 2019 was her last one. I had never been to one of these conferences, but I'd heard about it for the 11 years she was involved! I knew this last conference was a big deal, and this moment needed to be celebrated. This was the first of many losses for Mom. It was a great day and a well-deserved celebration.

Finding meaning during this challenging journey is another way to celebrate your loved one. I've added some ways to find meaning during your caregiving and more examples of how I do this with Mom.

- **Focus on the person:** While you are working at being present with your loved one wherever they are at, it's also important to remember they are so much more than their disease. That is why I tape pictures of Mom at different ages on my mirror in my closet, so I remember that she still has emotions, a diverse history, and a desire for connection.
- **Plan meaningful activities:** Cook a favorite meal together or flip through photo albums together. This has already been covered in this chapter, which validates the importance of this tip. Besides cooking meals and reminiscing with photo albums, I also like to do holiday-themed crafts with Mom to help reinforce the time of the year. It also provides some normalization for me. Mom used to love to decorate for every single holiday. In 2023, I noticed this wasn't happening anymore, so she and I have been doing this together now.
- **Share your story:** Sharing your own caregiving experiences and tips with others can help you feel more empowered and positive than disheartened. This was shared earlier in Chapter 2 when I discussed how the store owner, Marla, asked what my mom was like after I shared why I was buying purple pumpkins from her. There are so many ways to share your story. After each caregiving visit, I post pictures on Facebook of my weekend with Mom to share where we are during this journey. I like to wear my Alzheimer's purple T-shirts when I'm out and about. It helps me feel like I can be Mom's voice, which she no longer has.
- **Take advantage of resources:** The Alzheimer's Association is a vast source of resources for families and caregivers. From support groups to education on the disease to referrals for advanced care, the Alzheimer's Association is a tremendous support. I have reached out to some support groups for myself throughout my journey.

- **Use nonverbal communication:** Gentle touches, smiles, and eye contact are helpful. Mom and I hold hands wherever we go together. I lotion her hands often. We smile and look at each other frequently. We frequently sit on the couch beside each other without speaking. We have found different ways to connect as we do not have the conversations we used to have.

A final way to celebrate and find meaning in your caregiving is to respect your loved one and treat them with dignity. This may feel like something that doesn't need to be said, but let me explain further. When you are in the depths of caregiving, it may become mechanical and rushed. The constant repeating, the showering, the dressing, and the toileting may feel like something you just want to get done. It may feel like you're caring for an infant or toddler. But you cannot forget who you are caring for.

Even though I may not feel like Mom's daughter while doing these things, I am. I am my mom's daughter, and she is my mom. When dressing/undressing or showering my mom, I always ask permission and state what I will do next. "Mom, I'm going to take off your socks. Is this okay?" When I wash her, "Mom, I will wash your back. How does that feel?" "Now, I'm going to bend down and wash your feet. Is that okay with you?" Dignity. Respect. This woman raised me. This woman was a brilliant attorney. This woman went to Washington, D.C., for women's rights events. This woman cannot dress and shower herself, but I will not rush through these tasks and overwhelm her. I'm not going to argue with or correct her. I'm not going to dismiss her feelings. I'm going to give her eye contact down at her level. I'm going to use short, simple sentences. I'm going to give her time to process what I'm saying. I will try again later if she says no to something I'd like her to do. I'm not going to question her recent memory. I'm going to be patient, cheerful, and reassuring. I'm going to make her feel safe and loved. Because this is how all of Mom's care is, I believe that is why she is happy and agreeable most of the time. She can still feel emotions. If we come in rushed, irritated, and anxious, quickly taking off her socks and pants, she will feel that and may reject our help, feel unsafe, and be uncooperative.

We have been fortunate that, for the most part, Mom is agreeable, not irritable or combative. Some of you reading this may not be having this same experience. Alzheimer's disease presents itself in so many ways, and it's highly unpredictable. As I was nearing the end of writing this book in January 2025, we were just beginning to experience some irritation and rejection from Mom. Dad was getting pushback from her about going to ESSE, so he had to be creative and insistent to get her to go. On a few occasions, she refused his help to get dressed and wanted him to leave the room. We were noticing anxiety and irritation. The neurologist prescribed Xanax as needed. Dad finds that a Xanac an hour before going to ESSE, regulates Mom's anxiety and irritation and it's a smoother morning for both of them..

For those of you dealing with more difficult, irritable, and even combative behaviors, checking with your neurologist is always the first step. In addition, try creativity in how you approach your loved one. What works one day may not work the next. As caregivers, we must have many ideas and tools in our pockets. As my dad has learned, walking away from the room and giving Mom space sometimes helps her regulate. While you're trying all of these different approaches, always, always approach with dignity.

I can't believe I'm near the end of this book, and I haven't mentioned the TV show *This Is Us!* For those of you who have not seen the 6-year season yet (2016–2022), beware of spoilers coming. It came out on NBC in the fall of 2016. Mom also started watching it at the same time I did. It was on Tuesday nights, so during my car drive to work on Wednesday mornings, we always dished about the show together. We were all in! The show followed a family of 5 throughout their past, present, and future. We discovered early on (spoiler ahead!) that the matriarch of the family, Rebecca, is diagnosed with Alzheimer's. My heart sank a little as storylines with this disease are always hard for me to watch. However, we continued to be in love with the show!

As the show's seasons progressed, so did Mom's Alzheimer's. By the end of 2019, the back-and-forth of the story lines was getting confusing for Mom, and she was having a more challenging time

talking about the show with me the next day. By mid-2020, those next day's talks stopped, as did the morning phone calls. I continued the last two seasons without my mom.

In season 6, we see the adult children caring for their mom, Rebecca, who is now in the advanced stages. This season aired in 2022, and I hadn't started my caregiving visits for Mom yet. As I rewatch the show now (yes, I do that often!), one scene hits me much harder than it did 2 years ago. One of the siblings, Kate, is frustrated with the lack of connection that she's seeing between her brothers and their mom. One day, when the siblings are all together with Rebecca, Kate brings them both into the bedroom, where she helps her mom prepare for the day. She instructs her brother Kevin to lotion her hands and brother Randall to brush her hair. She encourages them to look at their mom—to really see her. To speak gently and lovingly to her while they're performing these cares. This scene could not have been done any better. That is the stuff of caregiving. That is the stuff of celebrating your loved one amid memory loss. That is the stuff of dignity and respect. I know I am drawn to this show for those reasons, along with it having been a special show between Mom and me. I rewatch the show to feel closer to my mom. I respect the way this show handled an extremely difficult disease.

While writing this book, my parents and I saw the movie *A Complete Unknown* in January 2025. It's a touching movie about Bob Dylan's folk-singing days, 1963–1966. Mom still does well watching movies, especially if they have music. This movie celebrated the years when my parents were in their 20s. I paid attention to Mom during the songs, and when the song "Blowin' in the Wind" came on, I saw her smile, and then her lips moved. I couldn't take my eyes off her. My eyes teared up, and I was just present with the joy and memories that she was experiencing during that song. By watching my mom, I was celebrating that moment when she remembered that song from her 20s. Anytime you can experience joy during this tragic disease, you must sit in it. Take it in. Celebrate it and carry it with you. (I do recommend this movie if you haven't seen it by the time you're reading this book!)

One last and obvious way I celebrate my mom is by writing this book. The process of writing this at the end of 2024 and getting it published in mid-2025 was therapeutic and comforting for me but also extremely exciting and profound. In mid-2024, after about 10 caregiving visits, my emotions were so intense, and I was struggling with what to do with them. When I processed with my therapist that I thought I had a book in me, I started jotting down ideas and even attempted an outline. During the process, I realized I didn't know what I was doing and was ready to toss the little work I had done in the trash. It suddenly felt too big, and who was I to think I could write a book?

A few days passed, and I found myself googling "How to write a nonfiction book." I will forever be grateful for what came up for me in my results and believe that it happened for a reason at this exact time in my life. The name Kelly Schuknecht and her e-course: "How to Write Your Book in 12 Weeks" popped up in my search. I thought a short e-course would be perfect for my schedule. I signed up immediately, and in early October 2024, I was starting her course. People who know me know what type of student I was throughout my school years. I'm still that person!

A week or so into the course, I started emailing Kelly with questions, and soon, that became a regular habit. As luck would have it, Kelly began to go out independently and start her own business during this course. Before I knew it, I was part of her start-up, "Author Power Circle." The Author Power Circle is a supportive community for professional women who want to write a book to promote their business or share a personal message. Led by experienced book coach Kelly Schuknecht, members meet weekly to discuss their book ideas, tackle roadblocks, and stay accountable to their writing goals. The group fosters encouragement, collaboration, and creative momentum, making it easier to push through the challenges of the writing process. Whether you're just starting or need motivation to finish, the Author Power Circle offers the structure and camaraderie required to see your book through to completion. Learn more at kellyschuknecht.com/author-power-circle.

As I participated in this, I was struck by how my mom would feel about what I was doing. Not only was I writing a book, but I had stumbled across a community of women empowering each other. Empowering women was so much of what Mom was about. While I was also sad (as I often am during this journey), I also felt so proud of myself because I knew Mom would be over-the-top excited about this. The irony is that for me to get to this point in my life, Mom had to have Alzheimer's disease. So, there was no way Mom would ever be a part of this process with me. However, I feel that with this new community of supportive women I've found, Mom is still with me.

I charge you with celebrating your loved one with dignity by using several strategies in this chapter, but primarily by caring for this person who once cared for you.

Reader Application:

- How do you celebrate the loved ones in your life?
- What does "finding meaning in a difficult situation" mean to you?
- Can you think of a time when you were treated with dignity?
- How did that feel?

NOTES:

Chapter 5

Self-Care for the Caregiver

"Sometimes you will never know the value of a moment until it becomes a memory."

—Dr. Seuss

It feels ironic to leave the self-care chapter for the end of this book, as that is how most caregivers prioritize themselves. Caring for yourself is one of the most important things you can do as a caregiver. According to the *American Journal of Alzheimer's Disease & Other Dementias*, dementia caregivers report "more chronic illnesses as well as a higher prevalence of physical symptoms, poorer self-ratings of health than noncaregivers, and poorer overall health . . ." Dementia caregivers also report "poorer mental health than the general population, and the mental health status for unpaid family caregivers is significantly lower than for paid caregivers." Caregivers commonly report fatigue, anger, and depression directly due to the demands of caregiving.

This chapter will provide 25 strategies (provided by CaringBridge) for taking care of yourself during this challenging journey. I will also share strategies Dad and I have used and what we could do better.

1. **Let go of guilt:** Let go of the notion that putting yourself first is wrong. You do not need to feel guilty or selfish about that. I worry more about Dad than myself in this category, as Dad is in it 24/7. The days Mom goes to ESSE are crucial days for Dad to get about

6 solid hours away from Mom. He often runs errands and pays the bills, but he also takes his nap time and TV time, which he enjoys.

2. **Join a caregiver support group:** Joining a group of people with whom to share a similar journey can help you feel less alone. There are online or in-person groups. The Alzheimer's Association and CaringBridge are great resources. Dad tried the support group through ESSE once, and I tried one through the Alzheimer's Association.

3. **Stretch and breathe:** This doesn't have to be a yoga class. It can be just finding a few moments in the day to take deep breaths, slowly exhale, reach up to stretch, and then come back down. I do this often in my job as a therapist and try to remember to do this when I feel tense during my caregiving visits.

4. **Get some laughs:** There are many ways to find laughs. Try calling your funniest friend or watching your favorite comedian. Laughter can improve your immune system, relieve pain, and even improve your mood. No wonder it's called the "best medicine"! A positive and interesting aspect of Alzheimer's is that those with the disease can say or do the funniest things! The three of us have so many laughs during my caregiving visits! It brings normalization and joy to our lives.

5. **Talk to someone once a day:** Staying social is vital for your overall health. Caregivers need someone they can vent to or be distracted by a topic that isn't about caregiving. Since my parents have lived in the same town for 50 years, they are well established in their church and have other friendships. Dad likes to talk on the phone, so this is a strong support for him. I discovered that he and I had also started this routine for ourselves, which has become a source of self-care for both of us. On the days he takes Mom to ESSE (always by 8:30 a.m.), I receive a text from him after dropping off Mom that reads, "*Mom is at ESSE.*" That is my cue to call him. We check in about drop-off and his plans for his "time off." It doesn't replace the calls I used to have with Mom,

but it is a new source of support and love that Dad and I have found in each other.

6. **Get rest:** Maintaining nighttime sleep consistency is so essential for caregivers. The challenging piece of this tip is that if you live with your loved one, this can depend on their sleep. Early in 2024, Mom was struggling with UTIs, which directly impacted her sleep and, of course, Dad's. They were only getting about 3 or 4 hours of sleep a night for a while. Luckily, Mom and Dad are both averaging much more sleep these days. Dad also takes a short nap or rests daily, even when Mom is there. Luckily, she is not wandering yet and always stays close to Dad.

7. **Prioritize nutrition:** Good nutrition becomes critical to maintaining your health and well-being. During these caregiving days, it can become too easy to turn to fast food and takeout. These foods can contribute to heartburn, depression/anxiety, and a weakened immune system. Dad is not quite ready to start using a service like "Mom's Meals," which can be sent to their home, but I keep a close eye on when more support in this area may be needed. During my caregiving visits, I always make a meal (with Mom's help, as mentioned in Chapter 4), which I know they don't make for themselves anymore. I make sure it's nutritious and a past favorite of theirs.

8. **Ask for help:** This seems to be a hard one for many caregivers. I know it's hard for Dad. I was so proud of him when, in October 2023, I presented my caregiving visit plan for 2024, and he agreed to it. He was reluctant at first to "put that burden" on me or "add to my already busy schedule." Once I started visiting, he felt relief and even depends on them now. Trying to do this alone will absolutely cause burnout.

9. **Start a CaringBridge site:** CaringBridge has an on-site planner that helps coordinate care and organize needs. Dad and I have not tried this yet, but we will keep that idea on our future needs list.

10. **Don't be afraid to say no:** Caregivers must prioritize what's most important and empower themselves to say no, as needed. Dad

used to travel to our home in Iowa more often than he can now. After he drove here in September 2024 for the Alzheimer's Walk, he had to say no to coming for family birthdays that October. While this is a loss for all of us, it's understandable and supported.

11. **Ask for flexibility at work:** Some caregivers are retired, but many are not. It can become difficult to balance work and the role of caregiver. As noted in Chapter 3, I had support from my job in January 2024, when I started my caregiving visits, and again in May 2024, when I changed jobs. Being able to be off every other Thursday and Friday helps me balance helping my parents in another state and still being home with my family for part of the weekends.

12. **Spend quality time with friends and family:** Doing this can bring joy and healing during these difficult times. I'm fortunate to have 5 of my best friends from high school who still live near my parents. On some of my caregiving visits, we plan dinners or simply just hang out. Just a few hours together provide a nice distraction for me.

13. **Take time for spiritual practices/meditation:** You can do this anytime to add peace to your day. Meditation has been shown to reduce anxiety and improve sleep. I try to practice this in the peacefulness of my office between clients, looking out the window at the pond, or simply enjoying my coffee. In addition, both Dad and I find comfort in our churches.

14. **Keep a gratitude journal:** As a therapist, this is something I encourage my clients to do, and I have been doing this daily since COVID began in 2020. Practicing gratitude can help rewire your brain to be more positive. You can also look back at it when you struggle to see the positive. Practicing gratitude can be done through a written book or a phone app. The phone app I often recommend to my clients is *Gratitude Jar* (an iPhone app). It's short and straightforward, and how you can "shake the jar" with the gratitude stars in it brings instant happiness!

15. **Find time for exercise:** Like stretching and breathing, exercise doesn't have to mean spending hours doing it! A good walk around the neighborhood counts and helps to relieve stress. Including your loved one in this can benefit them as well. Walking together is a huge part of my parents' routine. I have also added a walk by myself every Friday morning when I'm there during my caregiving visit.

16. **Reduce caffeine intake:** Too much caffeine can cause irritability, sleeplessness, and anxiety, all of which caregivers do not need. My dad has never been a coffee or big pop drinker, so that's a plus.

17. **Listen to music:** Music has been scientifically proven to reduce stress. You can add this when driving, cleaning, cooking, or doing pretty much anything. I created a special playlist for my drives to and from my parents' home.

18. **Treat yourself:** This could be tricky for caregivers, but it's important to do something special for yourself during your difficult caregiving journey. Once I started spending more time in my old room during my caregiving visits, I bought some fun things to put on my walls to make the room more like mine again.

19. **Make time for your hobbies:** Hobbies help contribute to your happiness. Many hobbies can be inexpensive and not time-consuming. Try to incorporate your interests into your daily life or weekly routine. This can be challenging for some caregivers, especially when the loved one cannot be left alone anymore. My dad has had to give up most of his hobbies over time, but he still enjoys watching sports and some favorite shows.

20. **Play with a furry friend:** Animals, especially dogs and cats, can bring joy, happiness, and support during challenging and difficult times. If you already have a pet, you can grab extra snuggles whenever needed. If you don't, take advantage of a friend's or family's pet. During the Alzheimer's Walk weekend, I witnessed Dad enjoying playtime with our two visiting dogs, Minnie and Harper.

21. **Read books:** Reading can be a nice distraction and help relieve stress. It can also be helpful for caregivers to read books that can offer support. I started reading more fiction books in 2024 to help with distractions when my mind was just too full. Frieda McFadden has been a good friend!

22. **Create self-love mantras:** A mantra is a word or series of words repeated frequently to help with a positive mind-set. Practicing this can help caregivers refocus their minds and increase strength. I often encourage my clients to do this and would like to improve myself.

23. **Consider professional help:** Besides support groups, individual therapy is also available as additional support. As a therapist, of course, I strongly support this strategy! I also have my own therapist, as I mentioned at the beginning of this book. Without her, this journey would be much more challenging.

24. **Don't make self-care another "to-do":** Not all these strategies will resonate with you. That's why this is a long list and a whole chapter in this book. Find a few things that work for you instead of what you feel you "should" do or others tell you to do. Self-care should not be a "to-do" but something you look forward to.

25. **Be kind to yourself:** Lastly, but most importantly, please go easy on yourself. The most important part of self-care is that you simply start thinking about your own care and not just your loved ones'. Be patient and kind to yourself while you figure this out.

In addition to that list are a few more specific mental and emotional self-care strategies. As caregivers, we can have such high expectations for ourselves. Then when those expectations are not met (which, when dealing with Alzheimer's and dementia, they often are not), we can be extra hard on ourselves and carry guilt around. *An essential tool is forgiving yourself when you don't get the desired result.* You may wake up in the morning with the goal of having the patience of a saint . . . until you're asked the same question 10 times in a row before breakfast. I have gotten irritated with my mom with the repetition of questions, and then guilt and shame shoot through my body. As caregivers, we *will* make mistakes and not always like our interactions with our loved ones, but we must learn to forgive ourselves and be gentle to ourselves.

Another helpful strategy is to *rethink what you can accomplish in a day.* We have talked about having routines, but that routine must be flexible because, with dementia, you don't know how the day will go. Don't set superhigh expectations for getting things done during the day. There needs to be some "go with the flow" with caregiving.

This next one is tricky. *Keep an open mind.* As this disease progresses, you may need more support for your loved one. Caregivers need to be careful about promising or having the mind-set that "we'll never need a facility" or "I don't want a strange person helping in our home." At the beginning of the disease, caregiving is manageable. With Alzheimer's, it's a guarantee that it *will* get worse. We don't always know what "worse" looks like, so keeping an open mind in your caregiving plan is so important.

We've discussed this next strategy before, but it bears repeating. *Honor moments of connection.* When you least expect it, you may have a moment that feels like your loved one is their old self again. Earlier, when I shared that my mom was taking care of my injured

ankle (but rubbing my arm), her attentiveness and caring made me feel like she was the mom she used to be to me. I was so present at that moment and loved every minute. Celebrate those times.

Taking breaks is the next strategy, and this bears repeating as well. Breaks can consist of hours, like when Mom is at ESSE and Dad has 6 hours to himself. Breaks can also be short, like when you need to practice breathing and step away from the situation for a minute.

Creating routines with your loved one can be helpful to you as the caregiver and to your loved one. Routines help Mom feel comfortable and occasionally help her memory. This also helps Dad, as she is somewhat familiar with their days and enjoys what they do. Their routine grounds them both. Mom and Dad always do their walk or drive in the morning before lunch. Afternoon is for a nap/rest time, and 3:00 p.m. is their favorite time of the day because it's time to watch *The Kelly Clarkson* show. Even on the days that Mom goes to ESSE, Dad picks her up in time for the show. Dad calls it "Kelly Time." Because this routine has been in place since mid-2023, Mom can remember some of it. She can still read a little bit of the clock and somehow knows (likely because of the routine) that they watch *The Kelly Clarkson* show at 3:00 p.m. If she and I are upstairs doing an activity, she keeps an eye on the clock, and when it gets closer, she'll allude to the fact that we need to get downstairs for the show. "Kelly Time" is self-care for Dad and engagement for Mom.

I have also found that creating a routine for myself during this caregiving journey has been comforting, grounding, and a source of self-care. As mentioned, I drive 325 miles on a Thursday and back 325 miles on Saturday twice a month. I found that stopping at the same rest area (that happens to be the World's Largest Truck Stop!) in Walcott, Iowa, doing a few minutes of shopping, purchasing, eating the same snacks, and listening to the *That Was Us* podcast brings me comfort. I have found a routine that I can count on (and control) during a journey that feels very much out of control.

These trips have taken a toll on me throughout the first year of 2024, and they will continue to do so. I'm finding it's important to care

for myself in any way that works. For me, it's buying gifts for others from the World's Largest Truck Stop! and eating sugar cookies at 9:30 in the morning! I also take a selfie of myself whenever I stop and share it with family so they know when I'm halfway to my parents' place! As a caregiver, you can find that taking care of yourself is acceptable and important. That sugar cookie (both ways!) has become important and comforting to me. Find what works for you, share it with others, and be proud of yourself for taking care of yourself.

Journaling is the process of recording your emotions, thoughts, and actions. In Chapter 3 of "Ambiguous Grief," I mentioned keeping

a journal as a coping strategy. I have kept journals on and off throughout my life. As shared earlier in this chapter, in 2020, I switched to Gratitude journaling. There are many different types of journaling that you can choose from. Here are 7 different styles that may help you to detail your memories, feelings, and thoughts.

1. **Personal or Diary Journaling:** This is the most private of all journals, sharing your reactions and emotions to circumstances. This journaling style typically involves sharing your feelings, doubts, aspirations, relationships, and life goals.

2. **Gratitude Journaling:** This journal can help you focus on the positive aspects of your life and effectively promotes self-contentment. I encouraged my clients during COVID especially to take up this practice since we were in such trying and uncertain times then. A gratitude journal can help improve your mental health, well-being, and happiness.

3. **Art Journaling:** This journal is like a sketchbook and helps you practice your creative expressions. You may not be journaling words, and you can use a variety of pens, paper, embellishments, and stickers to illustrate your thoughts.

4. **Reflective Journaling:** Keeping a reflective journal can lead to self-discovery and developing visions for the future. This type may be more instinctive and document whatever you are thinking at the moment. A reflective journal can help reduce stress and initiate mindfulness.

5. **Video Journaling:** If you don't enjoy writing, you can express yourself verbally instead. Video journaling can be therapeutic, allowing you to unburden and discuss relevant topics.

6. **Bullet Journaling:** Another alternative to writing is bullet journaling, which requires less writing than other journaling methods. This can serve as a planner to help organize personal aspects of your life, including to-do lists, goals, and milestones. You can also start with blank pages and create sections and boxes that fit your writing.

7. **Stream of Consciousness Journaling:** This journaling involves writing without a goal or prompt. It develops your skills and challenges you to write more. This journaling encourages self-discovery.

As I've mentioned throughout the book, Mom and I used to talk to and from my way to work once I had a cell phone in 2006, and she was retired. We spent about 14 years on the phone together. It was our routine, how I started my day. Sometimes, she would be on the exercise bike at the gym with Dad. Sometimes, she'd still be in bed if I was early, and she took it easy that day. Whatever or wherever she was, that's how I started my day. We also talked on my way home if it worked in her schedule. She was my car companion. During COVID, this became less and less due to me not having a commute for a while and her abilities declining. While I now call Dad nearly daily, and he often puts Mom on the phone, it's just not the same. For some reason, in the summer of 2023, I was really struggling

with not getting to tell her so many things that would enter my mind. So, I decided to start writing to Mom. I got a pretty journal with butterflies on it and started my "Dear Mom Journal." I write whenever the mood strikes me. I write it directly to her. "Dear Mom," "I love you, Mom," and "Love, Dawn" are always in the letters that she will never read. I started in August 2023 and continue today. I am now on my second "Dear Mom Journal." Somedays, my grief is too big to write, and I just sit with those feelings and write when I can. I've chosen a couple of entries to share. This can be a very effective way of expressing your deepest emotions directly toward a particular person.

Lastly, and challenging for many caregivers, is *when someone offers to help, say yes*. For many people, even in noncaregiving situations, it's hard to ask

Dear mom, 4-6-24
I crawled in bed with you this morning. You were still so sleepy. We were up so late. I cuddled you + we laughed + just enjoyed the moment. You asked what I had to do today + I said I had to go home + you asked "why"? I wish I had more time.
I wish so many things.
I love you, mom.
Love,
Dawn

Dear Mom, 1-14-24
I ordered a chain to go w/ this one necklace of yours that I asked dad if I could have. I can't wait to start wearing it.
A year ago I got my "love, mom" tattoo on my left forearm. I love it so much.
Facetimed you today + you're so excited I'm coming Thursday. My first of many visits home to be w/ you. Note to me: You are my 2024 focus.
I love you, mom.
Love,
Dawn

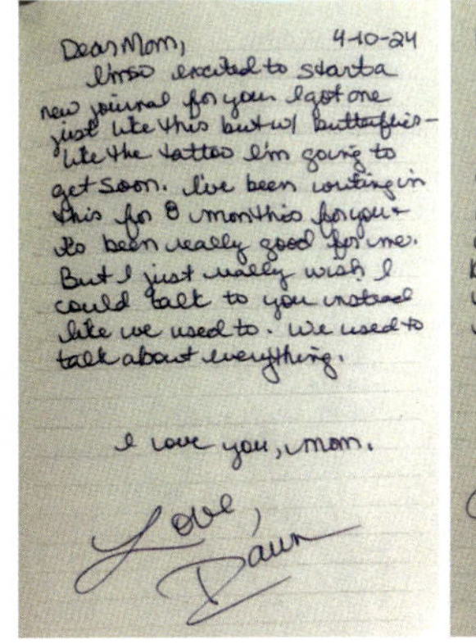
Dear Mom, 4-10-24
I'm so excited to start a new journal for you. I got one just like this but w/ butterflies - like the tattoo I'm going to get soon. I've been writing in this for 8 months for you + it's been really good for me. But I just really wish I could talk to you instead like we used to. We used to talk about everything.
I love you, mom.
Love,
Dawn

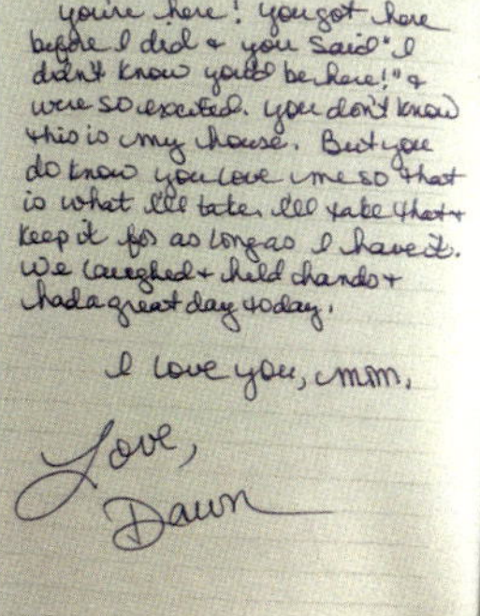
Dear Mom, 3-29-24
You're here! You got here before I did & you said "I didn't know you'd be here!" & were so excited. You don't know this is my house. But you do know you love me so that is what I'll take. I'll take that + keep it for as long as I have it. We laughed + held hands + had a great day today.
I love you, mom.
Love,
Dawn

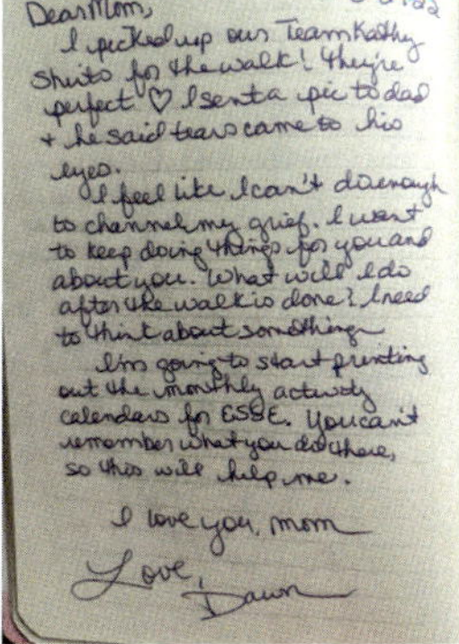
Dear Mom, 8-29-23
I picked up our Team Kathy shirts for the walk! They're perfect ♡ I sent a pic to dad + he said tears came to his eyes.
I feel like I can't do enough to channel my grief. I want to keep doing things for you and about you. What will I do after the walk is done? I need to think about something.
I'm going to start printing out the monthly activity calendars for ESSE. You can't remember what you do there, so this will help me.
I love you, mom
Love,
Dawn

for help. It makes us feel vulnerable. It makes us feel like we're not doing a good enough job alone. However, once help is accepted, the person often recognizes the benefits of this assistance. As I mentioned earlier, Dad was reluctant to agree to have me drive 600

miles twice a month to help him, but once I started it, he recognized how positive this was for him and Mom. So, he always says yes now.

Credit: NMK Photograpy

Reader Application:

- What does your self-care routine look like?
- After reading this chapter, is there anything you would change/add?
- Which type of journaling in the 7 examples provided might appeal to you and why?

NOTES:

Conclusion

Putting It All Together

"The next best thing to the enjoyment of a good time is the recollection of it."

—James Lendall Basford

Throughout this book, you've learned about the difficulty and complexity of Alzheimer's disease, why memories are important, what ambiguous grief is, how to celebrate your loved one, and how to take care of yourself, the caregiver. Throughout this book, I have shared my mom's story. I have shared all my emotions related to this journey I have been on with my mom.

I recognize that some unique parts of my story not all caregivers will have. While driving home from a caregiving visit in January 2025, I reflected upon the challenges of being a long-distance caregiver. I would see them more if I lived near my parents, but the visits would look different. For one, I wouldn't be sleeping over in my childhood room. I could stop by, check in, help for a bit, and return to my home. After each of my caregiving visits from Thursdays to Saturdays and the 325 miles each way, I require a "recovery period." This recovery time is both physical and emotional. Driving 1,300 miles each month on top of my job and other responsibilities makes me physically tired. Mostly, though, it's the emotional toll of spending solid days in a row helping with Mom. It's staying in my childhood room and recognizing

the enormity of changes that our family has gone through in the past 50 years. It's the realization of mortality and loss. It's the heaviness of responsibility and the never-ending love of two parents who have always been there for me. I believe that emotional toll led me to write this book. These emotions had to go somewhere. As I shared throughout my book, I tried some tools like journaling, therapy, exercise, and many others. Those helped, but I knew I needed something more, and this book became my "something more."

By reading about my personal journey throughout this book, you can now recognize that you want more for your loved one than just being happy and that memories do matter. You can identify different types of memories and state why they are important. You can use the term "ambiguous grief" to better understand the losses you are experiencing and feel validated. You have many ideas of ways to celebrate your loved one amid those tremendous losses. Lastly, you can recognize the importance of self-care and identify different ways that may work for you.

Now, it's time to change how you view your own experiences with caregiving for your loved one. You can accept all the feelings you are experiencing. You can recognize that it's imperative to express and share difficult and negative emotions with others. You can also begin educating those not on this journey with you. You can help replace the belief that "at least they're happy; that's all that matters" with "memories matter." You can share your loved one's past self while celebrating where they are now.

Throughout my journey, I've learned that it's okay to recognize, share, and experience my feelings. I'm not doing Mom a disservice by feeling my negative emotions and sharing them. The caregiver experience is part of this journey. Most books on Alzheimer's disease guide us on how to care for loved ones, which is obviously important. I believe the entire story is equally important. The whole story includes our pain, grief, anger, and sadness as caregivers.

Thank you for sharing my journey with me. Throughout this book, I've shared about the mom I had and the mom I have now. Sharing both matters. My 50 years of memories of Mom matter. I added many pictures throughout my story to help you visualize the woman she was and the woman she is with Alzheimer's. Her past and her present matter. It all matters.

My mom will never know I wrote this book for her and myself, but I can't wait to read it to her repeatedly. It'll be both painful and beautiful. That's my journey with my mom.

I love you, Mom.

Love, Dawn

A little bit more about who Mom was

Mom's Education History

Studied English language at Central Michigan University

- Mt. Pleasant, Michigan - Class of 1965

Studied English literature at St. Mary's University of San Antonio

- San Antonio, Texas - Class of 1968, Master's of English

Studied law at Northern Illinois University

- DeKalb, Illinois - Class of 1984

Mom's Work History

Taught English at a San Antonio High School

- San Antonio, Texas - 1966–1968

Taught English at Ann Arbor Pioneer High School

- Ann Arbor, Michigan - 1968–1974

Taught English at College of DuPage, Glen Ellyn, Illinois

- 1974–1980

Assistant City Attorney at the City of Evanston Law Department

- 1988–2006

Just a few more photos of the way Mom was

References

Alzheimer's Association. (n.d.). *24/7 helpline*. Retrieved October 10, 2024, from https://www.alz.org/help-support/resources/helpline

Alzheimer's Association. (n.d.). *Alzheimer's disease facts and figures*. Retrieved from https://www.alz.org

Alzheimer'sDisease.net. (March 23, 2021). *Stages of Alzheimer's disease*. Alzheimer'sDisease.net. https://alzheimersdisease.net/stages

Alzheimer's Disease International. (2023). *World Alzheimer Report 2023*. Retrieved from https://www.alzint.org

Alzheimer Society of Canada. (n.d.). *Managing ambiguous loss and grief*. Alzheimer Society of Canada. Retrieved October 20, 2024, from https://alzheimer.ca/en/help-information/i-have-friend-or-family-member-who-lives-dementia/managing-ambiguous-loss-grief

Alzheimer's Society. (n.d.). *Memory loss and dementia*. Alzheimer's Society. Retrieved October 20, 2024, from https://www.alzheimers.org.uk/about-dementia/symptoms-and-diagnosis/symptoms/memory-loss

Banner Health. (n.d.). *Why people with Alzheimer's disease might live in the past*. Banner Health Blog. Retrieved October 15, 2024, from https://www.bannerhealth.com/healthcareblog/teach-me/why-people-with-alzheimers-disease-might-live-in-the-past

CaringBridge. (n.d.). *Care for the caregiver*. CaringBridge. Retrieved November 11, 2024, from https://www.caringbridge.org/resources/care-for-the-caregiver

Connell, Cathleen. (1994). *Impact of spouse caregiving on health behaviors and physical and mental health status*. American Journal of Alzheimer's Disease and Other Dementias 9(1): 26–36. http://hdl.handle.net/2027.42/68204

ESSE Adult Day Services. (n.d.). *Our mission and purpose*. Retrieved November 1, 2024, from https://esseadultdayservices.org

HopeHealth. (March 15, 2023). *From a dementia caregiver: 10 tips for self-care*. Retrieved November 11, 2024, from https://www.hopehealthco.org/blog/from-a-dementia-caregiver-10-tips-for-self-care/

Indeed Editorial Team. (August 17, 2024). *10 types of journaling (with how-to steps and tips)*. Indeed Career Guide. Retrieved November 1, 2024, from https://ca.indeed.com/career-advice/career-development/types-of-journaling

Mooney, J. (December 2023). *Ambiguous loss: The grief is real*. University of Rochester Medical Center. Retrieved October 18, 2024, from https://www.urmc.rochester.edu/behavioral-health-partners/bhp-blog/december-2023/ambiguous-loss-the-grief-is-real

National Institute on Aging. (March 25, 2024). *Alzheimer's caregiving: Caring for yourself*. National Institute on Aging. Retrieved November 1, 2024, from https://www.nia.nih.gov/health/alzheimers-caregiving/alzheimers-caregiving-caring-yourself

Pfefferbaum, B., & C. S. North. (2020). *Mental health and the COVID-19 pandemic*. The New England Journal of Medicine, 383(6), 510–512. https://doi.org/10.1056/NEJMp2008017

Tuscan Gardens. (September 23, 2016). *Turning life into a celebration for your loved one with Alzheimer's*. Retrieved October 20, 2024, from https://tuscangardens.com/blog/turning-life-into-a-celebration-for-your-loved-one-with-alzheimers/

UpJourney. (March 21, 2024). *Why are memories important? (23 reasons)*. UpJourney. Retrieved October 20, 2024, from https://upjourney.com/why-are-memories-important

Your Support Services Network. (October 14, 2022). *Ambiguous grief—grieving someone who is still alive*. Your Support Services Network. Retrieved October 20, 2024, from https://yssn.ca/ambiguous-grief-grieving-someone-who-is-still-alive

Alzheimer's Association 24/7 Helpline

The Alzheimer's Association® 24/7 Helpline (800.272.3900) is available around the clock, 365 days a year. Through this free service, specialists and master's-level clinicians offer confidential support and information to people living with dementia, caregivers, families and the public.

A recent study found that people who make even a single call to the 24/7 Helpline experience improved mental health and are better able to manage emotions, access resources and engage in action planning.

Contact the Helpline day or night to:

- Speak confidentially with master's-level care consultants who can offer support, answer questions, help in a crisis, and provide information on issues people face every day.
- Learn about the symptoms of Alzheimer's and other dementia, such as vascular dementia, Lewy body dementia and mixed dementia.
- Find out about local programs and services.
- Get general information about legal, financial and care decisions, as well as treatment options.
- Receive help in your preferred language through our bilingual staff or interpreter service, which is offered in more than 200 languages.
- Dial 711 to connect with a TRS operator.

Our professional staff has the knowledge to address a variety of topics:

- Memory loss, dementia and Alzheimer's disease.
- Treatment options.
- Safety issues.
- Tips for providing quality care.
- Recommendations for finding quality care providers.
- Strategies to reduce caregiver stress.
- Legal and financial documents for future care.
- Aging and brain health.
- Referrals to local community programs and services.

A model of collaboration

The 24/7 Helpline provides nationwide service while delivering personalized response and local follow-up. An online knowledge bank and community resource database helps staff respond quickly and accurately to calls, providing disease information, caregiver education and local resources across the country.

A recent study found that people who make even one call to the 24/7 Helpline experience improved mental health and are better able to manage emotions, access resources and engage in action planning.

The Alzheimer's Association 24/7 Helpline is supported in part by grant number 90ADCC0001-01-00 from the U.S. Administration for Community Living, Department of Health and Human Services, Washington, D.C., 20201. Grantees undertaking projects with government sponsorship are encouraged to express freely their findings and conclusions. Points of view or opinions do not, therefore, necessarily represent official ACL policy.

Stages of Alzheimer's

Early

Alzheimer's symptoms are mild and characterized by general forgetfulness.

Symptoms include

- Forgets recently read material
- Trouble organizing/ planning
- Forgets where valuables have been placed
- Trouble managing money
- Forgets recent events, names, details about own identity, & dates
- Trouble with challenging tasks at work
- Wanders & becomes lost in familiar places

Middle

Alzheimer's symptoms are more disabling and additional care may be needed.

Symptoms include

- Delusions, compulsions, or repetitive behavior
- Agitation, restlessness, & anxiety
- Needs assistance with getting dressed
- Bladder & bowel function issues
- Trouble learning new things
- Problems with reading & writing
- Loses track of time or surroundings
- Sleep disturbances

Late

Alzheimer's symptoms are significant and apparent.

Symptoms include

- Significant personality & behavior changes
- Loss of ability to hold a conversation
- Difficulty moving, eating, & swallowing
- Loss of bladder & bowel control
- Lack of awareness of recent activities or surroundings
- Highly susceptible to infections like pneumonia

AlzheimersDisease.net

Caregiver Self-Assessment Questionnaire

How are YOU?

Caregivers are often so concerned with caring for the relative's needs that they lose sight of their own well-being. Please take just a moment to answer the following questions. Once you have answered the questions, turn the page to do a self-evaluation.

During the past week or so, I have ...

1. Had trouble keeping my mind on what I was doing.... ☐Yes ☐No
2. Felt that I couldn't leave my relative alone.................... ☐Yes ☐No
3. Had difficulty making decisions............................ ☐Yes ☐No
4. Felt completely overwhelmed...................... ☐Yes ☐No
5. Felt useful and needed .... ☐Yes ☐No
6. Felt lonely............................ ☐Yes ☐No
7. Been upset that my relative has changed so much from his/her former self............ ☐Yes ☐No
8. Felt a loss of privacy and/or personal time.................. ☐Yes ☐No
9. Been edgey or irritable........ ☐Yes ☐No
10. Had sleep disturbed because of caring for my relative....... ☐Yes ☐No
11. Had a crying spell(s).......... ☐Yes ☐No
12. Felt strained between work and family responsibilities... ☐Yes ☐No
13. Had back pain................. ☐Yes ☐No
14. Felt ill *(headaches, stomach problems or common cold)*...... ☐Yes ☐No
15. Been satisfied with the support my family has given me.............................. ☐Yes ☐No
16. Found my relative's living situation to be inconvenient or a barrier to care........... ☐Yes ☐No
17. On a scale of 1 to 10, with 1 being "not stressful" to 10 being "extremely stressful," please rate your current level of stress. ____________
18. On a scale of 1 to 10, with 1 being "very healthy" to 10 being "very ill," please rate your current health compared to what it was this time last year. ____________

Comments:

(Please feel free to comment or provide feedback.)

____

____

____

____

____

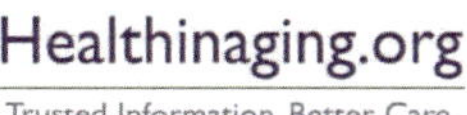

Self-Evaluation

To determine the score:

1. Reverse score questions 5 and 15.
   For example, a "No" response should be counted as a "Yes" and a "Yes" response should be counted as a "No."
2. Total the number of "yes" responses.

To interpret the score

Chances are that you are experiencing a high degree of distress if any of the below is true:

- If you answered "Yes" to either or both questions 4 and 11
- If your total "Yes" scores = 10 or more
- If your score on question 17 is 6 or higher
- If your score on question 18 is 6 or higher

Next Steps

- Consider seeing a doctor for a check-up for yourself
- Consider having some relief from caregiving (Discuss with your healthcare provider or a social worker the resources available in your community.)
- Consider joining a support group

Valuable resources for caregivers

HealthinAging.org
(800) 563-4916 | www.healthinaging.org

Caregiver Action Network
(202) 454-3970 | www.caregiveraction.org

Eldercare Locator
(a national directory of community services)
(800) 677-1116 | www.eldercare.gov

Family Caregiver Alliance
(800) 445-8106 | www.caregiver.org

Medicare Hotline
(800) 633-4227 | www.medicare.gov

National Alliance for Caregiving
(301) 718-8444 | www.caregiving.org

Local resources and contacts:

AGS/HiAF 7.24.2014

This questionnaire was originally developed and tested by the American Medical Association.

©2015 Health in Aging Foundation. All rights reserved. This material may not be reproduced, displayed, modified or distributed without the express prior written permission of the copyright holder.
For permission, contact info@healthinaging.org.

Now I will hold you, mom

January 1972

May 2024

Made in the USA
Columbia, SC
14 June 2025

14f87152-b46f-45cf-a574-970fdafedd7dR01